A Tall Glass of Water

Rehydrating the Dry Places Within Your Life

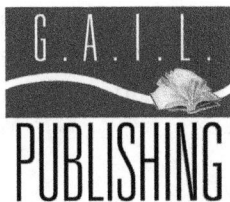

G.A.I.L. PUBLISHING

Published by G.A.I.L Publishing LLC

Book Cover Crea+ive Development Studios

Interior layout by
Anita Gillespie-Luckett | Anita's Designs & Events

Edited by Dieneke Johnson
Edited by Patricia Jones

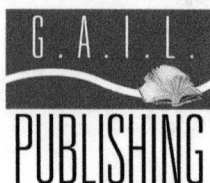

Published by G.A.I.L Publishing LLC
HUwww.gailcrowderinc.com

ISBN-10: 098321851X
ISBN-13: 978-0-9832185-1-7

Logo design by Marie Mickle

Disclaimer
Certain suggestions are made in this book. While these are intended to be helpful to the reader, the reader must assume all risk associated with following any particular suggestion. Therefore, in purchasing this book, the reader agrees that the authors and publisher are not liable or responsible for any injury or damage caused by the use of any information contained herein.

Printed in the United States of America

Acknowledgements

I would like to thank my Lord and Savior, Jesus Christ. Without you I could truly do nothing! I love you, Father!

To my husband; my best friend and the love of my life! Thank you so much for allowing me to be me! And loving me unconditionally!

To my two boys, Justin and Joshua; mommy loves you more than life!

To my mother, Sharron White; thank you for giving me wings to fly and words of wisdom to live by. I love you!

To my Aunt Clarice; thank you for teaching me your elegance and grace! I love you!

To my two brothers, Roger and Jeffery; it was hard growing up as the middle child and only girl, but God knew that I would need to learn to be tough and ready for life, so I thank you for teaching me to stand up and fight back in every area of my life. I love you both!

To my sisters, not by blood but by God! Kim, Joy, Judy, Val, Chris, and Evette; I love you guys. Thanks for all your support, ideas, love, laughs and tears and for telling me "No" when I wanted to do something crazy! All of you have been in my life over 15 years! WOW, what incredible friendships and sisterhood! I am truly a blessed woman.

To Kellie P. Easton; thanks so much for all you do for me. The list is limitless. Your business guidance is beyond your years. My business has grown and my brand is something to be reckoned with, because you got my vision and ran with it! I thank you from the bottom of my heart!

To Patricia Jones and Dieneke Johnson; thanks for helping me bring this book to life and getting it from my head on to paper. Without you I still would be writing this book! I love you both!

And to all the women who read this book use it to "Rehydrate dry places within your life."

Hail

Table of Contents

"Water is essential for life. Without water life would end. Without water life would never begin.

Water runs deep even when it's just a puddle. It's amazing how something so common can be so subtle."

– Justin Crowder

So think of the content of this book as water, to be sipped, gulped and drunk, thoughtfully and with intent, to bring your life into balance, and keep it that way.

WHO NEEDS THIS?

*T*his book is for women - for all the moms, single mothers and wives, the entrepreneurs, the sisters ... for any and all women who want it all. This book is for the women who have built businesses while their families suffered, friendships failed, and they made themselves sick with stress trying to get to that level of success they have been striving to achieve for so many years. Here is a tool for any woman who admits to needing help to put things in her life in balance – so that she CAN have a successful career, a happy family and meaningful friendships.

Sounds impossible? Take a sip. How can you possibly dedicate all the time your family and friends demand AND put as much blood, sweat and tears into your business, so that it succeeds? I am here to tell you that it is, indeed, possible to have it all – and I know this from personal experience.

This journey has been a very personal one for me. Before things were balanced in my life, I lived in a fog where my expectations were not realistic. I so much wanted this certain lifestyle that was just out of my reach. As part of that want, I also had set these expectations on my marriage, on my children, and on the people around me. I saw myself becoming this not so nice person. From the outside, everyone thought I was happy, but on the inside I was a mess. I internalized all this unhappiness and it became this internal struggle. I was literally out of whack. The best advice I've received so far in my life is to stop trying to correct everyone else's problems and mistakes, and to quit trying to live everyone else's lives – just find out who you are and be that, , and only that.

When I first started my business, my marriage, children and household suffered because there were only so many hours in the day that I could dedicate to either my business or my marriage and family. In the process, I was making myself sick and overworking myself trying to achieve my dreams.

Eventually I discovered that I needed to prioritize my life and utilize some of the advice that other people in my immediate circle had given me, so that I really *could* accomplish the goals I had set for myself. As a result, I have made it my business to give other women the tools and strategies that helped me put my life into balance, to have the best life that, deep down, I really wanted. I know it is possible to have it all – and to achieve the life you want – and I'm here to share that knowledge, along with some tips and tools, with you.

Go ahead: Take some sips, gulps and a big drink.

AUTHENTIC SELF

"Always be a first rate version of yourself and not a second rate version of someone else."
                                                    – Judy Garland

One of the most important things you need to discover is your Authentic Self. Once you discover who you are, you'll find that things will fall into a better balance. Stop trying to do things outside of your ability. Find out what you like to do and are good at doing – do that and do it well. If you are busy trying to pattern yourself after someone else, you may miss the opportunity of doing what YOU were meant to do. Having it all is not having all of someone else's dream.

Take a sip and ask yourself these questions:

What do I like to do?

Whom or what do I want to impact?

How can I do that within the space, time and resources within my reach and available to me now?

3

Once you find the answers to these questions in your own mind, embrace yourself, embrace who you want to be and where you want to be, because you will get there. You're always going to be a work in progress. As long as you acknowledge that fact, and are willing to be open to change internally, you will achieve that balance you need to get that happy, healthy life.

WOMEN'S ROLES AND ROLE MODELS

"The trouble with the rat race is that, even if you win, you're still a rat"

—Lily Tomlin

Take another sip.

*T*here was a time, not so long ago, when families had little choice but to decide to sacrifice everything if they were to earn the financial security they thought they wanted. The "American Dream" does not come cheap. It is not unusual for men and women to work fifty, sixty or even seventy hours per week on average. Some even work eighty or ninety hours, without giving it another thought.

For many individuals, their identities have become intertwined with their success on the job. Climbing the corporate ladder was, and is, an admired activity, no matter what it does to personal and social relationships. Meanwhile, the divorce rate is climbing, and stress related death and illnesses are on the increase. As part of that trend, more and more children are being raised in single-parent households than in the generations that preceded us.

Despite all this -- we foolishly believe that we are living THE life! Take a gulp.

If you are one of the enlightened few, you have already realized that giving up your family and your social life is not worth the price, just to have a successful career. Already you may be experiencing some stress-related health problems, or you aren't eating properly. Maybe you are fighting more and more with your spouse, your children, or best friend, because you are spending far too little quality time with them. Perhaps you find yourself not even having time to return phone calls, emails or text messages – let alone time to send out a card to someone you care about the most.

In today's crazy world, it is safe to say that you feel you don't have time for family, friends *and* work. And since your family and friends are not the ones who give you a paycheck to spend time with them, I bet that they are likely the ones to suffer, because work will end up monopolizing all your time.

TAKE A LOOK – AND A BREATH – AND A BIG SIP OF WATER!

"The be-all and end-all of life should not be to get rich, but to enrich the world."

–B.C. Forbes

*T*ake a minute – just a minute to look around...notice anything? You're not alone in this! Many people, in all types of jobs, are looking for balance, less stress and more time to spend with family and friends. The desire for work/life balance has become the number one goal for people of all ages in the workforce today.

The Baby Boomers and Forty-Somethings are cutting their work hours. Many Thirty-Somethings are starting their own businesses, just so they can have control over their own lives and schedules. Recent studies have shown that young people are choosing to turn down promotions/opportunities to achieve a greater balance between work and life.

Now, if you WANT more balance in your life -- but are wondering if it is all that important -- let's take a moment to discuss the reasons why you *NEED* this balance. It really is a necessity. Take a sip.

HEALTH

It's obvious – living an unbalanced life, where work dominates your time, significantly affects your health. Long and/or stressful hours can wreak havoc on your heart, body and mind. Long work hours also encourage a poor diet and leave little time for exercise.

Let's add it up: no exercise + little-to-no sleep + health problems = a person who is no longer a powerful asset to herself, her boss (or to her own company), nor can she participate fully in family and social lives. Does she look and sound familiar yet? Time for another sip!

Besides the physical health, there is the emotional wellbeing to consider as well. Your ability to give back to your family and friends depends on your own emotional stability –

which depends on a balanced life. Working long hours, day after day after day, leaves you little (if any) time to decompress and relax. Let's face it: After 10-plus hours at work, you're exhausted, but you know that as a wife, partner, mother, sister or friend, your day is not over when you walk out those office doors at the end of the work day. You're walking from one job to another -- the one you have at home. Your emotional reserves are depleted. You have no patience with yourself or others. You are short on sleep and even on time.

STRESS

Are you suffering from insomnia, tension headaches, rapid weight gain or weight loss, lower sex drive, or chest pains? Do you get sick a lot? Well – it may just be because you're stressed! Living an 'all work and no play' lifestyle has huge implications for your health – and STRESS is a factor all its own. You have to remember that work/life balance is not just a question of the hours you spend at one place or another – it's also a question of how balanced you feel and how you react to things. When you become less a victim of stress and overwork and take control of your own reactions to stress, you will live longer and will be happier at BOTH work and at home.

FAMILY AND COMMUNITY

Let's do a reality check (take a gulp!): This 'all work and no play' lifestyle affects a lot of relationships in our lives. Studies tell us that all 'work and no play' contributes to more divorces and more dysfunction in families and relationships. It can also contribute to lack of involvement and investment into our communities and neighborhoods. People and families struggle with the successful balancing of schedules. Often this can be the reason that the children fail to thrive emotionally and physically. If the family succumbs to divorce, single parents are even more stressed with even less time, which in turn makes thing deteriorate even more, creating a ever-downward spiral. As parents and future parents, we need, instead, to become role models for marriage and relationships, to show how to juggle and manage our time and our lives for future generations. If we do nothing to change we're just perpetuating the problems.

PRODUCTIVITY

It is a FACT that the human brain (yes, your brain) needs downtime, rest and recreation to function properly. Think about it: The last time you had to work long hours and get something done, I bet you found that you could barely focus after a awhile. Your mind starts to wander, you're thinking about other things, or you're zoned out – in any case, you are not with it. It is necessary to take time for yourself. Take a walk. Talk with friends. Do things that will help you regain your clarity and focus. By doing this you will spend less time reworking the things you've done wrong, mistakes you've made and the details you've missed. And in the end, you will get better quality and output. Take a sip.

For example: Have you ever been so tired that you found yourself just sitting at your desk, staring at your computer screen, but nothing really registered? And then someone walked up to you to ask if everything is ALRIGHT? That's when you know that you need to take a step back, get some fresh air, and regroup.

LIFE GOALS

Everyone has them. Goals. And you are no exception. You may have work and career-related goals, such as promotions, more responsibility, and wanting to earn more recognition. Those are fine and dandy, but you have to be sure not just to focus on your job. Many people identify their success in life by their promotion in their job and the recognition they get there – but what about the other aspects of your life? You are more than your job. Be sure to set personal goals, family goals and general goals in your life so that you can grow as a person and lead a happy life.

Let me give you a personal example. I love being on stage talking to hundreds of women around the country. But after I have taught my last class, and spoken my last message on relationships or fashion, more than anything else I want to hear from my children, husband, family, friends and others who have crossed my path, that I am a good person, and have made some measure of difference in their lives. Having my own business is great, but it is not worth losing my family and friends over!

CHANGE OF MINDSET

It's time to take action! (Take a gulp.) Now that we've talked (I've talked – you've read) the reasons why work/life balance is so important, you know that you are not alone! The question is: What do you do about it?

You may HATE what has happened in your life, and you may not see right now how to change it. You will be happy to know that you CAN change your life. Whether you make this decision for health reasons, relationship reasons or simply out of the need to get control of things – you have more than enough justification and motivation to make the move. Trust me.

It can only happen when and if you make a firm decision and commitment to make this change. Be realistic on how fast and how far you can go with your plan. Let's be clear about something: We are not talking about quitting your job and hoping that someone will donate money to your cause (because nobody will). There is a real difference between achieving balance in your work and family life and the idea that you don't have to work at all. Work is part of life, and it's healthy and constructive. It pays the bills; it gives us the reward of real accomplishment and the feeling of useful participation in the community and society. What we're talking about here is the rational balance of your work, home and social life – a balance that has become all too rare in today's world for many of us.

Go ahead and involve your boss, co-workers and friends in the process. Keep the lines of communications open and you WILL end up where you want to be. Sounds pretty simple – right? Well, depending on your age, and how long you've been in the rat race, you may find it slightly harder to make the change. With a bit of perseverance and the right support system, you can and will succeed.

Let's look at this scenario: You want to be able to attend your child's soccer practice every Wednesday at 4:00, but you don't get off work until 5:00. How about suggesting to your boss that you could cut your lunch time from one hour to 30 minutes on two days out of the week? You have not added to your office time (nor reduced it, which is important to your boss and your income!), AND you get to your child's games! Everybody wins!

"THE CAREER"
versus
"THE JOB"
(TAKE A GULP)

"Work expands so as to fill the time available for its completion."

—C. Northcote Parkinson

*H*ey-hey-hey – before you run off to tell your boss that you simply need more time off to spend with your family, or change your hours completely, you need to (and should) consider a few things. Do you have a contract that requires you to work certain hours? Is your position critical to the company? Does everyone in your company/department work crazy hours? Can you take another position that may have a lower stress environment?

15

Look at your position and determine if you have a "job" or a "career," a "business" or a "hobby." Take a sip. If you are in it for the long haul, and hope to climb the ladder to upper management or similar business success, you can expect to work much longer hours and endure a lot more stress. If the reason you are working really long hours and under a ton of stress is because your boss is nuts then you need to change jobs. But before you do that, be honest with yourself. Make sure you are not the one adding to the problem. Try to improve your relationship with your boss. If your own attitude and feelings of obligation about work are contributing to your long hours and are burying you, you have to make some changes in your work habits. If you have emotional issues about what is enough, or how to be well liked on the job, you have to address those. Some companies offer job coaches or life coaches to help you get through these obstacles. If not, think about getting a life coach on your own time, or go to a counselor and work through your issues. It'll pay off in the long run!

Don't forget – it is important to do a good job and even, many times, go the extra mile – but you never should put yourself in a situation where you are the only one shouldering all the work.

PLANNING CAN BE FUN! DREAM!

*H*ere are some simple tips to get your time under control. Take a sip! If you do these things, you'll find that, even in the most stressful and time-consuming jobs, you can reduce the hours you spend at work/at your office, and arrive home in a less stressed, and more family friendly frame of mind.

Personally, I like to do what I call a mind DUMP at the end of each day. This can be by way of a journal, a personal computer log, or a conversation with a friend or spouse. It helps to unclutter my mind. How? If I am talking with a person, it will take me probably less than a minute. I tell him or her how my day went, from start to finish, what I accomplished, and what didn't get done. If I am doing it in writing, I do the same thing, without worrying about spelling or grammar. Just stating it gives me the overview of what I did get done, and is yet to be done. Then you are ready to outline what's next. Most of us don't give ourselves enough credit for all the things we do get done in a day's time.

Make a "To-Do" List. Organize your list, starting with the most critical. Cross each item off your list as you complete them. If you don't finish the items towards the bottom of your list on that day, you add them to the list the next day – don't drop them!

Just Say "No." If your boss wants you to work late but you have a family engagement that same night, it is okay to say "no." You can suggest alternatives – like working late the following night or coming in early. Just don't be so quick to accept the request without probing to find out if there is another way to handle the situation. Protect your personal commitments!

Know Your Brain. If you are a morning person, attack the most difficult problems in the morning when your brain is the sharpest. That way you don't have to re-work the problem the next day when you discover your afternoon mistakes.

Get Enough Sleep. Your brain can operate on a short amount of rest for a day, but if you are not getting enough sleep consistently you will not think clearly or process information well. In the end you'll make mistakes and spend more time trying to fix them. More and more, lack of proper sleep is linked to serious health issues that affect every aspect of your life.

Advertise Your Schedule. If you have it on your schedule to make phone calls first thing in the morning, let incoming calls go into voicemail until you feel ready to take calls. Take the time to get your day organized and to have that first cup of coffee. You will feel more focused and get a lot more accomplished.

Be Your Own Time Master. Take a sip. Sit down with your calendar and figure out how to allocate your time. Schedule and plan your work activities and get your personal family obligations on that calendar. Treat your personal plans with the same respect you would treat a business meeting. Don't cancel your personal appointments unless it is a real work emergency. If you *have* to cancel reschedule immediately. Explain the reason why to your family member or friend, so they don't think they are unimportant to you. And be sure to keep your appointment with them the next time!

Be Present In The Moment. Don't spend time during a family dinner worrying about tomorrow's presentation. Put your mind back where it belongs. Let's face it – worrying has never helped anyone accomplish a goal. You are either prepared or you're not.

Don't Agonize Over It. Don't procrastinate because you don't like a particular activity. As a matter of fact, do the things you like the least FIRST – then reward yourself by doing the things you like to do most. Put things on your calendar and stick to those dates – don't talk yourself into putting things off, or you'll just have even more to do later.

Train and Delegate. Don't tell yourself you don't have the time to show someone else how to do that task that you *really* don't have to do yourself. Take the time to teach others, if they are available to you, and soon you will have a well-oiled team machine! When you don't have to do ALL the work yourself, you will find a lot more time to get other tasks done, still get out of the office on time AND get home for family time. There's another benefit to this time management technique: You can finally take that vacation or a long awaited three-day weekend and not have to worry about calling the office every hour to be sure there isn't some problem that only you can solve. Your family will appreciate having your time and attention, and everyone will benefit from that much needed bonding time, including YOU!

Get Organized. Take another sip! It is IMPOSSIBLE to manage your schedule if you can't find things or if you have to recreate or reinvent something because you can't locate it. Take this action item to heart – and start NOW! Put a task at the top of your list to organize files, or to rearrange things so they are easier to find. Once you have things organized, don't let them get out of control again. And just think: If you reorganize now, you'll NEVER have to go through it again.

Keep a Realistic Perspective. Setting unrealistic goals is a HUGE mistake. Whether it is the completion date, or a project, or the time you think it takes to deliver on something – if you underestimate the time required to get the work done, you will end up working late and you'll look bad and feel worse. Be realistic about when you plan to complete tasks and make sure you do your homework to know that you can accomplish the assignment in the expected timeframe. Consider other ways you can get the job done if you think that will help you meet the deadline faster. Just don't promise something that you can't deliver. It's good to set goals that challenge you, but if you can never reach the goal, you will not do yourself --or others-- any favors. We'll talk about your goals and what you really want in a little while, but for now, you'll need to think realistically about your dedication to balance your life. It will come with some sacrifices in certain areas, but it will reap many benefits to your life – health, relationships and happiness. Is balancing your work and your family life important enough for you to make some tough choices (If it isn't, you may not get the balance you want.) You need to **DECIDE NOW! START TODAY!** TAKE A BIG GULP!

KEEP THE HOME-FIRES BURNING!

"Work is the meal of life, pleasure the dessert."

– Bertie Charles Forbes

We've talked about the work environment and some of the adjustment you will need to make there. Now, we have to take a candid look at your family situation. Hey: Don't stop reading! Unless you are just starting a career, you probably have a lot of fence-mending to do – and that is okay. We'll set things in motion and get everything on the right path.

Your family and friends may be very discouraged and disappointed that you haven't found a way to spend more time with them. If this is the case, you need to talk to them and let them know them what you have in mind. Tell them you are going to dedicate yourself to achieving balance in your life and ask them for their input. More importantly, *listen to what they have to say*. Remember, you don't have to take every suggestion that comes your way, and make it clear that you will do what *you* feel is best in the end, but that you want their thoughts on the topic. Listen carefully, be true to yourself and be honest with your family and friends about what you hope to achieve.

ONLY PROMISE WHAT YOU CAN DELIVER

There should be no surprises. (Take a little sip!) **Before** you start this discussion, put some of your thoughts down on paper. Think through what you can achieve, realistically. Be prepared to talk to your family and friends and have some idea of how you will execute your plan. When you discuss these ideas with your family, be sure you preface your discussion by explaining that you want to change your focus and balance. Tell them that you know that work has been pulling you away and you want to change that. Just knowing that you recognize the problem and want to work on it will make them feel better. If you have children, talk to your spouse/significant other first before you call for a family meeting. Consider how you want to address the kids. Remember that children will often take what you say very literally, so don't play fast and loose with your language. Think carefully about what you want to say and don't forget: Only make promises to them that you can deliver. Don't lead them to believe that you are quitting your job or are closing your company to stay home with them and play all day. It is likely that whatever plan you design to regain some balance in your life will take some time to execute, so don't promise that everything will be fixed by tomorrow. The fact is that balancing work and family – in short balancing your life – can be a constant challenge. Take a sip.

TWO NEW "MUSCLES"

To help complete your plan, you'll need to develop two traits, or "muscles": *Self-discipline and Awareness.* Most of us have some difficulty with both of these, but if you concentrate on them to break the bad habits that distract you and take you away from what you really want to do, you will be much happier. Without self-discipline you do all the things that you shouldn't be doing, instead of spending that time with your family and friends. Self-discipline and breaking old habits go hand in hand.

Become aware of what you're doing and what you're saying. Every time you catch yourself taking things for granted, remember that the little time you have with family and friends is important, so pay attention. Don't fritter it away. Listen to what your spouse, child or friend is saying to you. Look for opportunities to grab special moments during the chaos of your week. Don't just slide through life.

MAKE IT HAPPEN, WITH RULES AND COMMUNICATION!

THE FIRST CONSIDERATION: RULES!

*P*erhaps you're thinking that you hate rules. Most people do, but they are a necessary part of life. Think about it! Laws are nothing more than societal rules that keep the wheels greased and running to prevent chaos. Rules also apply to when and how the family will get together to do things. Rules apply to YOU as they relate to when you'll come home from work and whether you will attend the Friday night movie with the family. (No more begging off because of your perceived work obligations!)

A good way to establish these rules is to have the family sit-down and develop a list. Everyone can vote and everyone's opinions count. Some rules may be simple and some may be temporary. With the set of new rules printed and posted on the refrigerator, you and your family will have a better idea of what to expect in certain situations. But don't expect the family to obey the rules if YOU don't obey them. You have to keep your end of the bargain too!

THE SECOND CONSIDERATION: COMMUNICATION!

To keep your life and family life in balance, you need to devote time and attention. But you also need communication. (Take a sip!) Even if your job is demanding, you can balance your life better with your family if you make them a part of the equation. If you say you are going to call at a certain time, be sure you do! Don't leave them hanging. Email or send text messages to keep connected. Agree on how and when you will communicate throughout the day – even when you are not home. This sets the expectation and keeps communication flowing. Tip: Create a mail slot or an "in box" for all the notices from school, permission slips and other items. A mailbox for each person in the family is even better, if you have space. You can leave little notes for each other to keep in touch, or just say hello, or "I love you."

FRIENDS ARE ESSENTIAL

How is Your Social Life? (Time for a sip.) While we are on the subject of your personal life, let's not forget your friends. Everyone needs them and everyone should have them. Friends are a necessary social extension: A group of like-minded people who share your values, though perhaps not always every opinion. They provide an outlet to let your hair down when you need to. Time out with friends, whether they are old high school buddies or friends you made at work, is important. See a movie, grab a cup of coffee, have an occasional dinner, perhaps even share an activity like bowling, golf, sports, book club, and/or see a show at a theater or ballet. All of the techniques we talked about for your family life apply also to your friends. Above all, keep in touch. Schedule events and get-togethers with a realistic eye to what you can achieve. Put the appointments on your calendar just as you would any business meeting, and be faithful about keeping the appointment, even if it seems a guilty pleasure during the critical crunch season at work. If you absolutely must cancel, communicate clearly and let them know you have to reschedule.

DO reschedule. Don't leave it to chance or you will never get together. When you do meet, don't talk shop, or you will not get away from the stress you tried to leave behind at the office. It is a hard habit to break, and it may take some time to focus on this new habit. Make it a game – by agreeing that the person who breaks the 'don't talk shop' code first has to buy a round of drinks or coffee or has to pay for dinner.

Woman does not live by work alone! While your family is very important, your friends offer a different perspective. They are often more honest with you than your family can be, and they will forgive and forget because they don't have the same intimate emotional attachment of a spouse, mother or a brother. You can count on them to make you laugh and to share your successes and failures. They are part of your psychological armor and a necessary part of your life's balance. Seek out friends actively and don't be afraid to invite a new friend for a drink or coffee. There is no harm done if the friendship doesn't blossom. Friends make you more interesting and expand your horizons. And, believe it or not, they keep you from becoming a boring 'all work and no play' type of gal. Again, you have to be disciplined, have a plan and pay attention, to take advantage of these opportunities to develop new friendships.

The five different types of friendships/relationships!

1) Your cheerleader

2) Your prayer warrior

3) Your tell-it-as-it-is

4) Your fence straddler

5) Your know-it-all

THE PROS AND CONS

1) **The Cheerleader**

   Pros – She is always saying you can do it! She never gets in her own game but is always in your corner, hoping and wishing that you will do well! She will make you feel good, even when you know (and she knows) you have made a bad call!

   Cons – She never really has anything going on in her own life that you can cheer her on with, or anything that you can help her out with! So you feel kind of bad for her, because she is living life through you!

2) **The Prayer Warrior**

   Pros – She will always have a word from the Lord for you! When you need a scripture and can't even think about what book it's in, she can lead you right to it! If you are having a bad day, she can pray you through just about anything.

Cons – She always wants to preach to you when you just need someone to listen to what you have to say.

3) **Tell-It-Like-It-Is**

Pros – She is your friend until the end! She is going to be in your corner no matter what. She will get down and dirty with you. She always has a shoulder for you to cry on.

Cons – She is somewhat loud, and doesn't usually think before she speaks. She has no filter on, and you never know when and where she will let loose.

4) **The Fence Straddler**

Pros – She likes to make sure that she doesn't hurt anyone's feelings, so she tends to go with the flow! She just to wants to be with you on your journey, but won't really get involved with anything difficult.

Cons – She can never help you make any tough decisions. She will sit back and watch what happens and then jump on the bandwagon when things have blown over.

5) **Your Know-It-All**

Pros – She has a big, bold personality, she's a mover and a shaker! She is in the know on all things! She likes to be in the spotlight and does not mind sharing it with a few close people in her circle. She likes to connect people that she feels can help her with her goals and dreams.

Cons – She is always busy and has a story to match yours! But, of course, hers is more dramatic! She is loud and needs to be seen and heard in all conversations! She has convinced herself that she owns the room.

NOW THE WORK BEGINS

(TAKE A BIG GULP!)

"Work is the greatest thing in the world, so we should always save some of it for tomorrow."
                                                                —Don Herold

Expectations. Up until now we've only touched on expectations, but they are possibly the most important part of your balancing plan. They come into play in so many ways.

Let's get one thing clear: These are YOUR expectations. Not your husband's, not your friends', not your children's or family members' – but yours! So what do you expect to get from a more balanced life? More free time? A closer relationship with your spouse/friends/family? Time to pursue a degree or to pick up a new hobby? Maybe you want to learn to ride a horse! Any or all of these are fine goals, but keep in mind that some of these plans may take MORE time away from your family, at least in the short term.

First thing first: you have to get it straight in your own mind. What does "balance" mean to you?

Is it more time for yourself? More time with family? Don't make a promise to get more work/life balance and then squander that opportunity with poor planning. What do you expect to achieve? How will this balance change your life? Also consider this: Are your expectations realistic for the planned timeframe and actions you want to take? Once you have your own expectations firmly in mind, how do they relate to your employer/business and your family and friends? Be fair to yourself and to others.

Setting Specific Goals. Like any other important decisions you have to make in life, you have to set goals, or else it's like shooting in the dark. To set goals for your life balance, you have to take your expectations and translate them into the 'what' of what you want to achieve and the 'when.' Be as specific as you possibly can!

Here are some ideas to get you started:

"My goal is to be listed as one of the Top Ten Women Entrepreneurs by May of next year."

"Reduce the number of hours I work by 10 hours per week so I can spend more time with spouse/kids."

"Visit my family every Sunday for at least three hours."

"Schedule and keep a weekly date with my best friend for a dinner and a movie."

Remember, keep them simple and specific! That way you can measure your success easily. The next task at hand is to figure out HOW to achieve your goals. Remember to keep your expectations and goals realistic or you will never get to where you want to be!

Here are some ideas to help you get started (take a gulp):

Time Management Tips

"Time is the coin of your life. It is the only coin you have, and only you can determine how it will be spent. Be careful lest you let other people spend it for you."   – Carl Sandburg

1) **Write things down** -- A common time management mistake is to try to use your memory to keep track of too many details, leading to information overload. Using a to-do-list to write things down is a great way to take control of your projects and tasks and keep you organized.

2) **Prioritize your list** – Prioritizing your to-do-list helps you focus and spend more of your time on the things that really matter to you. Rank your tasks into categories using ABCD prioritization.

3) **Plan your week** – Spend some time at the beginning of each week to plan your schedule. Taking the extra time to do this will help increase your productivity and balance your important long-term projects with your more immediate tasks. All you need is fifteen to thirty minutes each week for your planning session.

4) **Carry a notebook** – You never know when you are going to have a great idea or brilliant insight. Carry a small notebook with you wherever you go, so you can capture your thoughts. If you wait too long to write them down you may forget. Another option is to use a digital recorder.

5) **Learn to say no** – Many people are overloaded with too much work because they over-commit; they say *yes* when they really should be saying *no*. Learn to say *no* to low priority requests and you will free up time for things that are important to you.

6) **Think before you speak** – How many times have you said *yes* to something you later regretted? Before committing to a new task, stop to think about it before giving your answer. This will prevent you from taking on too much work.

7) **Continuously improve yourself** – Make time in your schedule to learn new things and develop your natural talents and abilities. For example, you could take a class, attend a training program, or read a book. Continuously improving your knowledge and skills increases your marketability, can help boost your career, and is the most reliable path to financial independence.

8) **Think about what you are losing out on to do your regular activities** – It is a good idea to evaluate how you are spending your time. In some cases, the best thing you can do is to stop doing an activity that is no longer serving you, so you can spend the time on something more valuable. Consider what you are giving up in order to maintain your current activities.

9) **Use a time management system** – Using a time management system can help you keep track of everything that you need to do, organize and prioritize your work, and develop sound plans to complete it. An integrated system is like glue that holds all the best time management practices together.

10) **Identify bad habits** – Make a list of bad habits that are stealing your time, sabotaging your goals, and blocking your success. After you do that, work on them one at a time and systematically eliminate them from your life. Remember that the easiest way to eliminate a bad habit is to replace it with a better one.

You can probably think of additional ideas, but this work kit will give you some notion of the considerations involved with every single goal. For every goal you set, you'll have to think about how reasonable the goal is, how achievable it is, and how exactly you plan to accomplish it in the timeframe you have set for yourself.

Be honest with yourself (and with each other) and, by all means, include your support network in the plan. When it comes to the goals of your family and friends, the emotional attachment and desire to do the right thing may make it hard to think clearly and to accurately plan for how and when things will happen. Ask your family to come up with their ideas about how you can accomplish these things. Brainstorm, and leave the door open for some crazy stuff! You will be surprised at what you might uncover that way. After that process, sit down and sift through the plan, to see which ideas are practical and which ones can be discarded.

As you start to put your plan in motion, be sure to review it occasionally to make sure that you are still on target and decide if you want to change anything. You have permission, remember?

BECAUSE LIFE HAPPENS! (TAKE A GULP!)

Let me say that again: LIFE HAPPENS. And you may have to change some of your timetables and tasks to incorporate the unexpected changes in your life. That doesn't mean you won't get there. Just knowing you have a contingency plan will keep you afloat and trekking forward. REMEMBER! PLAN is not just another four-letter word!

COMMUNICATION IS KEY

"Life is the continuous adjustment of internal relations to external relations."
                                                    –Herbert Spencer

We talked just briefly before about communication when we discussed family issues – but let's go just a little bit deeper. In general, communication will help you balance life and work by establishing clear boundaries and expectations with others. Exchange information with others and find out how they do things. You may learn a better or faster way to get things done, thus freeing up more time to accomplish the other things on your plan.

41

Oh, and don't forget: Communication is a two-way street. Be sure that YOU understand the priorities of the people around you (spouse, children, friends, employees, etc). If you understand how others think and feel you can offer to pitch in and help as needed. Surely this is a favor they will gladly return the next time YOU need help.

Communication isn't just talking. It's the whole two ears and one mouth principle (take a sip!): Most of what you'll learn and use to get things done comes from listening to what others are telling you. Test for understanding to be sure you actually heard what you thought you heard and interpreted it correctly. If you practice these skills you'll have a significant advantage in your personal and professional relationships. No matter how little time your family has together each day, if you are really talking to each other and listening to each other, you are making progress in creating balance in your life and in your relationships. Ponder that for a moment! If someone in your circle feels valued and important with your undivided attention, you are well on your way!

TIPPING THE SCALES

"There is time for work. And time for love. That leaves no other time."
—Coco Chanel

If you can't yet afford to make major changes in your career or your life to get the balance you need and want, there are some other ways to decompress and capitalize on the time you DO have for yourself and your family. By making some simple changes, you will at least FEEL like you have more quality time for yourself. Don't let life run you over. Get control. GRAB control! Know what you have to do and get it done. Then, when it is time to transition from work life to your personal life – and back again, you will be ready for the transition. To accomplish this, you need to think of your 'work time' and your 'personal time' as existing in two different worlds.

Each of these 'worlds' requires different skills, and a different focus. But each is very important. Let me give you some ideas that will create a 'transition' ritual for yourself – one that will get you out of one world and ready for the other:

- Get ready for things the night before. Don't wait until the chaos of the morning to do simple things (i.e. packing lunches, ironing clothes, preparing your briefcase, etc).

- Set your alarm and get up on time so you don't have to rush. Try getting up before everyone else if you think this would help. That will give you some extra quiet time, to have (and enjoy) a cup of coffee or tea, and a chance to write out the list for the day. Setting up a morning routine (and sticking to it) will help you feel less rushed and will set a nice tone for the day. It may take a few times to get it right, so be patient with yourself and members of your family.

- Use your commuting time – by train, by car or bus – to read a book you enjoy, make a list of action items for the day and/or to listen to your favorite music or radio talk show.

- At the end of the day, don't forget to transition back to your 'social, or personal' world. Switch out of the work mindset and use your time in the car, train or bus to reprogram yourself. Consciously leave behind the work worries, make a short list of items to remember for the next day if you need to do so ... then ... let it go!

- When you get home – remember: HOME should be a place of refuge, a soothing place, where you can be with those you love and care about, to get away from the problems of the day. It's okay, though, if you are having a really tough day, to ask your family and friends for a few minutes to regroup before you join in. As you

COPING WITH STRESS. (TIME FOR A SIP!)

Perhaps the most pervasive and difficult problem in life balance is stress. Whether you are at home or work, there is most likely some stress in your life, and that stress can interfere with your enjoyment of your career and your social life. We all understand that stress is what we experience when we must adjust to the constant and conflicting demands of our lives. For most of us, when we experience unrelenting stress -- and we don't know how to cope -- it will make us angry, frustrated, irritable, depressed and tired. It may cause us to get headaches, develop ulcers, intestinal disorders, or even to suffer from insomnia. Unless you learn how to eliminate or at least mitigate stress, you will function poorly in your businesses, at home with family and with friends.

Just acknowledge that stress is real and that it can affect your health, your happiness and your relationships adversely. There are a lot of ways to conquer stress, and you'll need to find the right ones for yourself. How does it figure into your life goals? By recognizing that there are different kinds of stress, it isn't all bad news. There IS something called positive stress, and something called negative stress.

Positive stress is what you feel when you're planning an event or when you're about to make an important presentation – a sensation of butterflies or excitement. You may be happy about the event and looking forward to the occasion, but that doesn't mean there is no stress. That kind of stress is not harmful and can be quite invigorating and exciting. Negative stress, on the other hand, IS harmful, especially if it's happening over long periods of time. The fight-or-flight response of your body releases adrenaline, which prepares you to confront immediate danger. When that response is extended, the result can be damaging.

So, go ahead – start by identifying the stressors in your life, and look for areas where you feel the most stressed. Then address the source of the stress – if you can, because, I'm telling you, the best way to approach stress is head-on.

The clues are not so hard to find. Notice the emotional and physical responses you have to stress. These could be tense muscles, headaches, nausea, grinding teeth. Don't try to pretend it isn't an issue – be objective about your reactions. Next, figure out what you can change and how you can relieve or eliminate the stress. Can you take those tasks or situations that cause you the most stress and schedule them in such a way that you can tackle them when you are fresh and rested? Can you shorten the time you are exposed to stress? Try to keep meetings and appointments short or try to schedule things during times of the day when you are less likely to feel harried.

If you have times of the day or situations where you are unavoidably under a lot of stress, try to take a break. Go for a walk outside or go get a cup of coffee. Break the pattern and then come back feeling refreshed to finish the task.

If you focus on making the necessary changes to avoid or alleviate the stress you will hit the problem at its root cause instead of trying to run and play catch-up all the time.

Another approach is try to analyze and alter your own reactions to stress. So much damage done by stress is not done by the event itself, but instead by your body's reaction to the event. Your body and mind perceive danger and react accordingly, and everything becomes exaggerated. The danger seems more threatening, the task more daunting, and the outcome more uncertain.

Don't obsess over what can possibly go wrong and predict failure. Stick to the positive and, even if things didn't go perfectly, focus on things that worked well and note them. THEN revisit the places that didn't work out so well, with a more objective eye toward improving the process, without taking or placing blame. Just be sure to learn from your experience, so you will do better next time.

Remember that you have the power to change your reaction to the stress. You can use exercise to mitigate stress, and you can use techniques like deep breathing, meditation and yoga as a way to relax the mind and body.

KEEPING IT FRESH AND FLEXIBLE (AND TAKE A SIP!)

As with any plan, your plan for your life balance must be kept fresh and flexible. Be sure you allow for contingencies and guard against backsliding. Old habits die hard, and you may find yourself in need of a refresher to stay on track. Remember that nothing goes just as planned, so be ready for the unexpected and don't let it get you down.

Look at your plan often and keep talking about it with your friends and family. The more you reinforce its importance to yourself and others, the less chance you will fall back into your old ways.

Let me say it again: Don't be discouraged if you hit a snag. It will take a while for the world around you to catch up. Even if many people around you may not understand the need for balance, the fact that you do may save your life and your relationships. If they fail to recognize the importance of your efforts and laugh at you for your choices, remain secure in the knowledge that you are running a marathon – not a sprint -- and that in the end you will finish the race well! You may be breaking new ground. You may become a role model. And, that position is not always going to be easy. Pioneers have hard work to do, but they ARE the first to see the beauty of the new horizon.

So, the point is – stick to your plan! You will become better at this as your old habits die. Remember to exercise that self-discipline and have the courage of your own conviction. Evaluate if someone else's request for your time and attention is aligned with your plan, and decide accordingly. Keep the plan and the perspective fresh and if one thing doesn't work, try another. It is your commitment to the change that is important. Things may not turn out exactly as you expected, but keep your focus on the goal of balance. Don't hesitate to get advice from others you trust if you get stuck along the way. You don't really have to do this alone.

Hey! Are you still here with me? We've gone over A LOT, and you may want to review this information again to make sure you got it all. The concepts are simple, and although you may find yourself wondering if all of them relate to your life balance, you will find the answers as you set the steps we outlined here in motion.

Try this:

1. Sit down with a pen and pad (or with your computer) and gather your thoughts and expectations.
2. Talk to your family, friends and employees to get their thoughts.
3. Then set your goals!
4. Make the plan and move forward.
5. Adjust the plan along the way if needed and don't forget to be realistic about what you can accomplish and how long it'll take.
6. Keep the lines of communication open and keep people informed about your goals and your progress about what is important to you.
7. Learn to manage your time better so you can leverage the newly gained free time to use as you wish.
8. Schedule and keep commitments with your family and friends.
9. Find ways to improve your productivity and learn how to transition from work to home and back again.
10. Don't get distracted!
11. Exercise self-discipline and stay committed.
12. Learn how to handle and diffuse stress and eliminate it from your life whenever you can.
13. Be optimistic and positive.

14. Understand that that work/life balance is key to your health and happiness and it can actually make you more productive at work and give you a better quality time with your friends and family.

And so…it's now your turn to get that plan on paper!

YOU CAN DO THIS!

"I don't want to get to the end of my life and find that I lived just the length of it. I want to have lived the width of it as well."

–Diane Ackerman

Take control of your life and live it to the fullest.

Keep your priorities straight!

Remember: You don't live to work – you work to live!

Find yourself, love yourself and change from the inside. Know who you are and know what you're not; know what you're working on in terms of yourself. No matter your age, you are still growing, changing and evolving. Just like they tell you on an airplane to put your oxygen mask on first before helping someone else, fix yourself first. Do it for yourself. Set milestones. Journal your progress. Go at a steady pace and use the tools and strategies in this book to help you get there, with the full glass of water now empty!

AFFIRMATIONS

I am my own best friend.

I deserve to pamper myself often and to nurture my desires.

The more I care for and love myself, the more love I will experience from others.

I claim my feminine power now.

The love in my life begins with me.

I love and appreciate myself.

I am a divine, wonderful expression of life, and I am living fully from this moment on.

I am my favorite person.

I love myself totally now.

I am happy, healthy and complete.

I am always learning and growing.

My income continuously expands. I prosper wherever I turn.

I always find time to be creative. This fills my spirit with joy.

Happiness is at the centre of my world.

My spiritual beliefs support me and help me to be all that I can be.

I know that everything that happens in my life is perfectly orchestrated. I am deeply fulfilled.

Whatever happens in my life, I know that I can handle it.

I am always safe and divinely protected and guided.

Everything I need to know is revealed to me. I am open to receiving this information.

Everything I need comes to me in perfect timing.

Life is a joy and is filled with love.

I am radiantly healthy.

I attract good into my life.

I am willing to change. I embrace change.

All is well in my life. I am at peace.

I am discovering how wonderful I am.

I see within myself a magnificent being.

I am wise and beautiful.

I love what I see in me.

I choose to love and enjoy myself.

I am my own woman.

I am in charge of my life. I expand my capabilities.

I am free to be all that I can be.

I have a great life.

My life is filled with love.

I appreciate each moment in my life now.

I am a powerful woman. I trust in my power.

I am worthy of love and respect.

I am free.

"Water is essential for life. Without water life would end. Without water life would never begin.

Water runs deep even when it's just a puddle. It's amazing how something so common can be so subtle."

–Justin Crowder

www.ingramcontent.com/pod-product-compliance
Lightning Source LLC
LaVergne TN
LVHW021545080426
835509LV00019B/2857